BIG WORDS FOR LITTLE PE

Helen Mortimer & Cristina Trapa

Learning

OXFORD

UNIVERSITY PRESS

Explore

As soon as our eyes open in the morning we are explorers, ready to notice new and exciting things all day long.

Discover

Looking, listening, touching, tasting and smelling allow us to discover more about the world around us.

Can you find the five senses here?

Help

Today you might
need to ask for help.

I can't find
my peg!

Tomorrow you might be able to help someone else.

That's why learning is easier when we work as a team.

Grow

We should make time every day
to think, to read and to imagine.

These things all help our minds to grow.

Questions and answers

Finding out answers always starts with asking questions. Never be afraid to be curious.

Solving problems

When we experiment, we find ways to fix a problem.

Technology

Using technology teaches us important skills and it makes learning fun!

Focus

Some things are hard to do and we need quiet time, without interruptions, so that we can concentrate.

Ssshh!

Try

It feels scary to try
something for the first time.

But when you believe in yourself and have others to cheer you on, then it's easier than you think.

Again, again!

Learning useful things by heart means that we remember them. They can help us every day.

Ready

When our minds are open and we are willing to work hard, learning is as easy as one, two, three!

Learning

From the moment we wake up to the minute we fall asleep, every day of our lives, we are always learning.

Ten ideas for getting the most from this book

1 Take your time. Sharing a book gives you a precious chance to experience something together and provides so many things to talk about.

2 This book is all about how we learn. Have you learned anything new today?

3 It's also a book about language. Ask each other how you would put learning into words.

4 The illustrations in this book capture various moments at a nursery or pre-school. We've intentionally not given the children names – so that you can choose your own and perhaps invent something about their personalities. What name would you give to the little dog?

Chadwick?
Titch?
Marnie?
Rusty?

5 Asking questions helps us to learn. 'Why is cheese smelly?' 'Why do we sleep?' Why not ask each other some questions and then try to find out the answers together.

6 Each spread shows a snapshot of learning in action. You could talk about what might have happened before and after each moment that's captured in this book.

7 Learning isn't just something we do at school. Learning can happen anywhere and all the way through our lives. Even grown-ups have to learn new things!

8 By exploring and recognizing the many different ways in which we learn we hope this book will give children and the adults in their lives the tools they need to make sense of the world around them.

9 Encourage curiosity – perhaps you could make a scrapbook together of all the things you would like to learn more about.

10 You could each choose a favourite word about learning from the book – it will probably be different each time you share the story!

Glossary

by heart – when we know something by heart, we remember it easily

concentrate – when we concentrate, we think about only one thing

curious – being curious means wanting to know or learn something

experiment – if you experiment, you try lots of different ways to find something out

technology – things we can use to help us learn